The hidden world of the London Underground

By Amy Frances H

Dedicated to my late father Bob Hammond

*

My mother Carol Hammond, sisters Louise, Eve and brother Brian

*

My delightful nephew and niece Jacob & Connie

*

My beloved Grace and Martha

TABLE OF CONTENTS

Contents

PREFACE

I have had the pleasure of joining the London underground mass commuter migration that occurs within the London Underground Monday to Friday, week in week out. I have observed the best and worse in human nature. I have been cooked in a metal can (known to most as a tube train!) in the height of summer and frozen in the same metal can in the middle of the winter.

I can say though it's a fascinating world that exists underneath the streets of London.

This book will tell you the good, bad and ugly of travelling on the London Underground and a lot more about human nature!

It will fill you with laughter and astonishment; some parts will make you recoil in horror. All have been based on real life observations; some have been embellished to encompass my active imagination.

All regular underground commuters will empathise and feel at one with the contents of this book.

INTRODUCTION

I would like to say a BIG thank you to all the people who form the great commuter migration that makes the London Underground so fascinating from 'oh my god did you just do that' to the 'oh my god how adorable' and the 'oh my god surely the human body cannot take being in a metal carriage with this heat without cooking' 'it would be legal to transport animals like this', then back to 'oh my god how disgusting!!'.

An underground world where we all try and style it out in front of a captive audience of sullen, dispassionate, detached, apathetic, mix of miserable human beings. One of the most common times we will witness this is if and when we do something that so is not part of the commuter 'persona', you know when you get your hair trapped in the door and stand there trying to style it out as if it was a new way of styling your hair whilst on the move, and why not? The travelling public seem to be of the opinion anything can be undertaken on the underground, from makeup, to cleaning their nose. I have seen someone using the underground carriage as a toilet and watched their pee run all the way down to my feet.

We all know the saying 'what goes on tour stays on tour' or in this case the underground!

Until now......

I would also like to thank all the people who both travel and work on the London Underground on a daily, weekly, monthly, yearly, lifetime basis! To the people who make this strange behemoth underworld continually operate, the cheerful or cheerless people who coax, cajole, and manoeuvre us all along like a lioness chasing and herding a wildebeest of people along the platforms, through the turnstiles, down the escalators into the tunnels and onto the train carriages; They tell us not to stop, to move along, to get on the train, to not stand in front of the yellow lines, to keep moving and to use all available space (when there clearly isn't any apart from the gap above everyone's heads and the carriage ceiling), to keep to the right or move to the left, to stand on the right and pass on the left. (which after years of practising this move we may now have to stand on the right and stand on the left when exiting on the escalator; I mean how confusing will that be to the commuter population!?), to not leave any items on the platform (does this include small children and your elderly parents, dogs, cats and budgies?), to not lean on the doors though you have no choice because you have been pushed and squashed tightly up against the very doors you are being told not to lean on, to wait for the next train despite the fact the one you are trying to force yourself on is the one that is going all the way to your station and the next five trains are not, to mind the closing doors, to avoid the gap between platform and train (difficult if you are in a very restrictive pencil skirt or you are one of those lads who think they are bang on trend and your trousers are down at your knees so we can all get a good look at your underpants seriously how on earth do you manage to walk when the waist on your trousers is around your knees? Do you have to practice this move because the only movement available is from the knees down like some small child desperately wanting a wee!)? Let's not forget about when we are told to squeeze up and use all available space (even though everyone steadfastly stays put so you have to pole vault over everyone's heads to get to all that free space between the seats) You are onto a winner if you are tall enough to reach the hand rails in this area or are lucky enough to get to that sticky central pole bang in the middle of the seating area (why are they always sticky? Boogies probably, have you seen how many people like to go fishing up their nose on the London underground?). If you fail to achieve either of these you can do what everyone else does and stick to the door area; the area that everyone is too afraid to move from because you never know, they may not be able to exit at the stop that is 2 hours away, so they steadfastly refuse to move into that free area in between the seats, no matter how much pressure is being piled on when that extra person squeezes themselves on to the carriage; fifty people, all with the 'I WILL NOT MOVE from this door' mentality, are all squashed together whilst one sensible individual is swinging around in that free area. Seriously, I love it because I am generally the one swinging around in that free area so I have no issues with everyone else supporting freedom of choice and choosing to get squashed up in others arm pits and other bodily areas just to stay near those doors.

People on the underground are like a species from another planet, they are a mass of pale sad looking beings who have one focus only and that is, getting to their destination in the shortest and quickest route possible and god help anyone if they get in the way, or in the way of whatever item they are carrying on their back, fore arm, hand or pulling behind them.

Experienced commuters just hate those dawdling idiots who plod and amble about, mainly looking confused or just shell shocked as this mass of people descend into the under belly of what is called the London Underground. That fabulous behemoth that just becomes part of your very being if you are lucky (most would say unlucky) enough to become part of that massive commuter migration we all call rush hour. During which time you are rammed against strangers you would rather not get acquainted too, where you see things that should only take place in one's own bathroom; where you curse (quietly so as not to be heard) at the bumbling idiots who block the fastest route to your chosen path because they haven't a clue where they are going or worse, they are 'walk reading' (nobody has mastered the art of speed walking whilst reading a paper, book or mobile phone).

You smell things you would rather not, you sweat in bodily crevices that you never knew existed, all because no one believed it would be nice to treat the beings of the underground to some air-conditioning when it is 1000 degrees in those carriages (think hot tin can in a furnace and you are in the tin can!).

THE STORIES

The silent chatting to oneself

It is amazing how much you end up chatting to your inner self it's like a new language of, 'oh for ffffffffff sake', 'MOVE', 'oh god not a suit case', 'are you serious',' IDIOT', 'cretin', 'moron', 'no way', 'oh my god put it away', 'don't get that hair over me', 'wow what are you wearing'? 'Oh my god I can see your knickers' (it goes on and on and on). The sad thing is it continues now when I am no longer under the streets of London!

You end up with this insane ability to talk to yourself constantly

'Oh my god why did they bring THAT on the underground'?

'Oh my god why would you wear six-inch heels and expect to be able to walk down those stairs'

'GET OUT OF MY WAY you cretin'

'Oh why on earth would you bring a small child into the life of the rush hour on the underground? At least wait until it starts work'

'Oh how utterly disgusting'

'Oh really! Please wear a longer skirt some of us truly do not want a view of your pants, or worse your bottom!, whilst you go up the biggest steepest escalators on the underground, ok maybe some guys do but seriously surely it's far too early in the day for any of that nonsense!'

'Oh look at that child. Isn't it adorable, and look its smiling at me'

'Oh how absolutely adorable, I want to sit next to the dog'

'Shut that racket up, I really do not want to listen your conversation'

'Do you not realise you idiot; your phone is on speaker so we can hear both sides of your conversation' - it was stuck to their ear at the time.

'Why would you wear sandals in the winter?'

'Wow you look great'
 'Oh shit that person has a suit case get out of my way! How can I get round them without just pushing them out of the way? Quick, quick there is a gap in the oncoming human traffic go, go, go'
'Oh please walk faster, stop your chat or move over so we can run past you'
'Now what's the strategy to deal with this idiot in front who is slowing the commuter traffic up? Maybe slap the back of their head and say idiot stop reading that paper because we would all like to walk faster than a snail's pace?'
'Just because you decided to carry on reading between platforms or exits or answering emails on the go, believe me it just doesn't work. You may think you can multitask but seriously you can't otherwise you would be trying to run like the rest of us behind you'
'Oh god please get out of the way love birds, seriously stop your marauding and blocking the zillions of commuters directly coming up behind you. MOVE OUT OF THE WAY, move aside and stop blocking the walkway!'
'Yuk please put her down and get a room for god sake, it's far too early for that'
'Shit they have stopped BRAKE NOW! Oh crikey too late' - As I run into them knocking them over and then I have to stop and make lots of polite noise whilst dusting them down, meanwhile everyone surges passed.
'That food just stinks and looks disgusting'
'God I am starving, and you have to sit next to me with that gorgeous looking food it smells great'
'DO NOT let any of that crap (skin makeup hair) go on me. Why don't you do that at home? Just get up earlier instead of inflicting that debris on the rest of us'

'Oh shit that human surge is coming my way!! Am I the only one going in the wrong direction? Quick against the wall NOW!'

'You smelly creature there is no excuse for not having a wash before you impose yourself on the rest of us'

'I can clearly see you are picking your nose you disgusting creature' 'oh so now where do you think you are going to wipe that?!'

Your thoughts can transpire into reality; thank you to the lady in front who put into practice my thought process when some man (moron) pushed me out of the way in his rush to get to the platform and I debated whether to deploy the sly kick action. She manoeuvred this action with precision and accuracy beyond me, after he did precisely the same and shoved her out of the way. We experienced commuters all know this sly kick the one just below the ankle which when skilfully enacted, the person receiving the kick is uncertain if it was by accident or deliberate (do not try this unless you are an accomplished sly kicker you may end up looking like a right idiot as you floor the person you applied the kick to and then proceed to trip over them). On this occasion he looked back at the deliverer of the kick accusingly but dare not say anything because they were unsure if it was deliberate or an accident. The low blow kick to this boffin was perfect and well deserved and made me smile all the way to work.

The stupidity of others

To everyone who thinks it's perfectly fine to deliver that emergency stop, right in front of the galloping herd behind you to answer that text message or change that one tune that you cannot stand, I salute you for your stupidity. I have yet to see these people get their just deserts, which would involve being peeled off the floor because the galloping herd behind you did not recognise your obvious stop sign.

Those adorable moments (they do happen!)

Thank you to the man who bought his assistance dog on the tube; what a delight to watch her face filled with such kindness and calm. She filled me with joy by just looking at me with those big brown eyes. I have yet to have the same reaction to anything other than a cute dog or kid. The commuter population rarely (in fact NEVER) have that kind expression accompanied by a look of sheer delight.

Thank you oh thank you so much, to the young man who sat next to me on the train with his friend's young bulldog puppy, Macy. Oh my god she was just a dream and so well behaved. The most courteous little lady ever! Everyone instantly fell in love and started to smile across the entire carriage. Hey, I bet there is many a person who would just love to get this reaction every time they got on the London Underground. A carriage full of beaming smiling happy people what a joy! What a rarity!

The effects of the underground to one's health

My immune system is top notch now because I have touched every hand rail, they would, if tested be harbouring the type of diseases normally contained in a laboratory, or there will be some sticky substance that you know may be the debris from someone's nose. If you are lucky, it will ONLY be someone's sweaty hand!

I have the underground to blame for the excuse, that my deteriorating eyesight has nothing to do with advancing age but everything to do with reading either my kindle, smart phone or paper two inches from my face because that's preferable to looking at some strangers crotch or bottom. Absolutely anything is preferable to gazing at another person's buttocks.

Those thank you moments

Thank you for all the adverts placed on the underground at least I can read them over and over and over again because it is so much better than making eye contact with anyone. The one time I smiled at someone he then spent the next twenty minutes chatting me up! My stop could not have come sooner! At least in a bar you are not surrounded by disinterested commuters who suddenly decide a love story may just be about to unfold in front of them or they are silently laughing at your obvious discomfort.

Thank you to the person who dropped £20 on the underground, I gave that to an elderly lady randomly in the supermarket that evening and to the person who dropped a £10 on the carriage I popped that into the collection box for the Nepal flood disaster upon exiting the station. I would have gladly returned it to its rightful owner however it was easier to pick it up than shout 'who's dropped £20' and getting trampled in the rush to reach it first and claim it.

Thank you to all the people who bring their children on the underground because we all then know its school holidays and there is hope (we can all live in hope at some point) that the underground will be less busy and just maybe we will get a seat for the entire journey not one stop from your station.

Thank you to the underground lift operator wishing us a 'Happy Thursday one more day to go hang in there before Friday', then loudly pronouncing 'HEY you sneaking in the other way I got you there it will NOT be happening again ! 'Let's make everyone's day and let that extra one person in the lift'. You made a usual miserable commuter community all smile. A magnificent feat in itself I can tell you!

Thank you to those empty underground carriages with seats available which gives me the opportunity to gaze out of the window instead of someone strangers' crotch, bottom, bag, paper, phone, book, in fact anything but the window. I discovered after two years of undertaking the same journey, that I travel past wormwood scrubs every morning and evening

Thank you to the female tube driver who in a clear very loud Jamaican accent said, 'REMOVE yourself from MY doors PLEASE!' Everyone on the entire carriage laughed, so well-done lady you got a reaction from the miserable lot in carriage four.

Thank you to anyone who gets on the carriage with flowers; it makes such a pleasant change to smell the roses instead of the various bodily odours that can be emitted from a human (in fact I am not always certain some of them can be from humans!)

Thank you to the kind gentleman (not) who thought whilst everyone was exiting the underground carriage you would try and get on. This really wouldn't have been a good idea at the best of times but especially not whilst I was in between the rushing herd coming out and you. Your lack of thought that maybe, just maybe, I did not want to get on that particular underground carriage ensured I got on the wrong train, such manners!

Blessed be for the newspapers we all grab at the entry to the underground, for keeping us all entertained and riveted with your stories; oh and those lovely pictures that you just have to smile at no matter how hard you try not to because you know someone in the carriage is bound to see you and think she's obviously mad. An example of this which springs to mind is the picture of the young Orang-utan holding a banana leaf over its head to keep the rain off was just so delightful. How could anyone not smile?

Thank you for shocking me into becoming sharp and alert first thing enabling me to take swift action to avoid a disaster!; I managed to avoid the idiot, who just around a sharp blind bend towards the exit, had decided to stoop down and with great leisure do his shoe laces up. Mercifully I deployed the actions of a swift divert like the ones you do to avoid a collision on the M25, knowing that if I had not, the hordes coming up behind may not have the same sense of attention and focus. I carried on at rocket speed knowing the squatter doing his laces up is just about to get pulverised, by what seems like the entire adult population of the UK, as they all descend on the London Underground together in their haste to get home

Thank you to the gaggle of excited primary school children who got on the underground at peak morning rush hour (your teachers were either incredibly brave or just plain stupid). Your excitement made me smile the entire journey. You were absolutely delightful. This excitement will disperse upon reaching adulthood when you become a 'commuter' undertaking this journey, day in day out, year in year out until you retire.

Thank you for allowing me to learn ten languages, write five books and read one million copies of those fabulous newspapers they throw at you at the entrance morning noon and night, a trillion books and a zillion adverts. My speed-reading skills are second to none. I am also now as blind as a bat because we commuters have to hold said reading material an inch from our face because someone's body part or backpack (carrying the kitchen sink) is a centimetre from smacking your left cheek ......warning to all commuters, reading that close it is BAD FOR YOUR EYE SIGHT!

Thank you to the underground for enabling me to become a supreme athlete without having to spend money on gym membership or make any additional effort to attend the gym. Due to the miles I cover on the underground, I can run with the best of them, and I can power walk to blast away fat as fast as it lands on any part of the body; walking the length and breadth of the stations connected through the London Underground network, up and down the escalators, darting through the slow paced walkers, running to catch that train on the platform even though you know there is another right behind, standing for hours upright through your journey unless you are lucky enough to get that seat which normally only seems to appear just before your stop.

Thank you to the thong of people who alighted me at the station; it was most helpful of you to be so kind and help me off the train in your haste to get off like a herd of buffalo. I mean it was most generous of you even though I had no intention of actually getting off at that particular stop!

Stair way to heaven

Oh and thank you so much for deciding to maintain the lifts just as I come into the station each day; now I have a choice: the wait and get pushed and corralled into the one lift that is in operation by the very cheerful station attendant or climb the zillions of steps, which seem to go on and on (surely with that many steps they must lead to heaven?). So if I choose to wait for the lift I will hear the lovely attendant asking us to squeeze in, politely asking us to 'go on push up, put you bags at your feet, make room for that extra person', regardless of the fact that you are already knee deep in someone's chest or are already trying to breathe through someone's armpit. However, it is impossible to do anything other than to keep smiling because the station attendant is just being ever so nice when asking.

My other choice is to take those stairs which surely aren't that hard to walk up? The very large sign at the foot of the stairs proudly tells you there are 120 steps; this will either put you off or make you feel proud and bigger than everyone who is waiting for the lift because you took on the challenge.

When you are brave enough (or stupid enough) you decide to take the challenge so you stride up thinking I am god I can do it! Then after about step 20 you think what the!!! By step 30 you are panting, by step 40 you are panting, sweating and hurling yourself up by the rail, by step 50 you are delirious with fatigue and by step 60 you are laid out gasping for water and a cool fan.

By step 70 they have called emergency services!!! Or that's what you would like, the fire brigade to come and rescue you...when you finally come round that final corner you compose yourself because you want everyone to see you when you stride out of the stair well like a top Olympian!! Smiling until you reach the office where you head straight to the medical room, collapse on the bed and remain there all day recovering.

Of course, this does not relate to me because I just run up those 120 stairs like they were nothing, flying over all the debris of the poor souls

I arrive at the top like an express train full of power and energy, looking like a super model without a drop of sweat, my attire in place and my hair looking like I had just exited the saloon. I swipe through the turnstile with my ready and posed payment card with a flash of the hand and I am outside in triumph like a hero ready for the next challenge.

Strategic Plans

The regular commuters amongst us will define a strategy to be deployed for the daily journey; these plans include placing yourself strategically so you have the quickest exit from the carriage, or the smartest route to your next underground platform. It's like a military plan to ensure that you have the shortest route to the lift so with dogged determination you will be strategically placed to enter the lift and also exit the quickest. For example, if it is a front load back exit lift you want to go straight to the back. If it is a front load but front exit , you don't care who is behind you, you are going to immediately bag the very front side and will stubbornly refuse to move just so you get out that door the quickest; flying to the exit barrier payment card ready and posed. Your strategic plan will also include where to stand on the platform to gain an exit advantage, and which carriage to alight - you pray for no obstacles such as, wheelie anything, children, tourists, drunks, old ladies, who are going to delay your journey through the London Underground labyrinth

Those barriers

We salute those entry barriers you fly through when you swiftly and stealthy pass your payment method across the reader and you curse those entry barriers that stop you in your tracks should it not accept your payment method. Often the first you know of this latter scenario is when you are smacked in the stomach and depending on your height, you may end up in a heap the other side wondering where you are. Even worse, you could be steamrollered through the now stationary barriers, by the force of the herd of people rushing directly into the back of you. The sudden impact propelling you through the likely broken barriers, with such force you end up out on the pavement, hand still posed with your payment card.

The other option is your card just did not register due to lack of funds and everyone lets you know what a 'dickie' you are stopping them going about their business at record speeds because you FORGOT to top up or you bank decided enough was enough on the bank overdraft. 'OH the embarrassment' as you manoeuvre yourself away, head down, card in hand or you shout 'oh for god sake, my stupid bank forgot I had money in my account'!

The Newbies

Oh my god, how easy is it to spot the underground newbies totting around in heels and clothes suitable for the catwalk? You may even remember, in the very distant past what it felt like to be an underground newbie, you know back when travelling on the underground was an adventure of exploration and joy? It is easy to spot the underground experts, they are the ones who are travelling at the speed of light in their flat shoes or very scruffy trainers (so 80s ladies) and dark clothing (light clothing will be black by the time you get to the office, it will be covered in soot and god knows what human debris YUK. You don't see it on black!). The seasoned commuter wears clothes that you can speed walk in (tight skirts - don't do it ladies nor 6-inch platforms, unless you are looking to break your neck).

The sensible amongst us do not wear any skirts above the knee or some floaty number because we all know what happens here don't we? The ride up the escalator provides everyone with a spectacular bird's eye view of your underwear if you were lucky enough to remember to put some on in your rush to get out of the door!

There should be a public warning on acceptable clothing on the underground; 'wear big pants at all times' it's windy down there and those floaty skirts will end up round your head; 'too tight a skirt below the knee and you won't be able to avoid the 'avoid that gap' exiting the train because your skirt won't allow you to step over it you will stop mid-air before dropping like a lead balloon down the crevasse between the platform and carriage'.

Or perhaps just a public warning that states 'Avert one's eyes whilst ascending up the escalator especially before one's breakfast!'

We all try to prove what a seasoned commuter we are, don't we? Demonstrating how we never lose our balance, we just go with every jolt and we can spot a newbie just by how they cling to those hand rails not knowing how greasy they are (more so in the heat of the summer) with those zillions of invisible bugs.

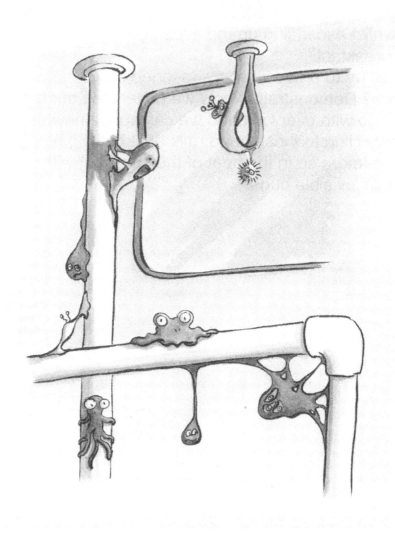

They will be scrapping the residue off their hands for years after.

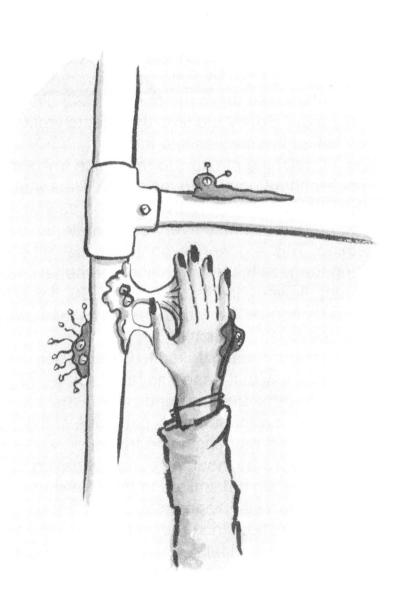

The Teachings

Thank you for teaching me how to contain the effects of a cold and all that goes with it. I really do not want to be that person forced into quarantine because as you sneeze or blow your nose everyone will be thinking 'oh for fffffff sake that's me done. Those dirty germs are coming my way!' So, by the time they get to work they have already talked themselves into the flu!

Thank you for teaching me how to relinquish my own personal space without going into meltdown. Personal space? THERE IS NO SUCH THING as soon as you enter London Underground because every cubic meter is taken up by something. This is generally someone else's body part or clothing, bag, suitcase (the bigger the better), tool kit, baby, dog, pram, flowers, the list is endless. So, if you are likely to go into meltdown if any of these items take up your own personal space, stay at home!

Oh and thank you for teaching me to be as miserable as I possibly can, you know that dead pan face look we all get as soon as we enter that underground zone. Trust me it's not the same on the overhead trains, everyone smiles, and people are polite, good mornings, and friendly acknowledgements. It's as though we are overtaken by the underground zombie, do not smile and avoid talking at all costs, stay in your own little zone unless someone jogs you out of it or you lose a shoe, trip up the stairs, fall down the stairs or your payment card fails. Then and only then it's like a light bulb goes on and you become human again for those few minutes.

Oh and for teaching me how to balance on my two feet whilst the train sways or undertakes an emergency stop all because some idiot has leant on the doors (this is an essential skill for all on the underground; you want to avoid touching those hand rails at all costs!) and then when I failed to remain upright I can make it all look so graceful when I fall head first into at best, a seat, or at worst into someone's lap!

Thank you for teaching me how to control my emotions because some of us are very happy and keen to keep things private whilst travelling on the London Underground; others seem to think they are in their living room, at home or worse still, in their toilet at home and we know what goes off in there don't we?! I now know how to contain pain if I bang myself or if one of my fellow commuters dumps their not so light bag or suitcase on my feet, or someone stands on your feet and has not noticed/doesn't care that something is beneath their foot and often with considerable weight. I on the other hand am quietly screaming YOU STUPID PRAT, you are on my foot! All the while trying not to draw to much attention to myself by causing a fuss or enlightening everyone to my plight, I quietly smile (through pain induced gritted teeth) and say 'excuse me but could you ever so slightly move your weight, bag, suitcase, tool kit towards the left because my foot (or other body part) is underneath?' When really you want to say, 'oh for fffffffff sake get your foot, bag, suitcase, blasted tool kit OFF ME you stupid blithering idiot!'

The Tourist

The only people who do not become underground zombies are the tourists who chat, laugh and joke amongst themselves and even more so when they are packed in like sardines. They seem to enjoy the thrill of being crushed into someone else's body parts and they NEVER move away from the door, clutching to that area like their life depends on it because god forbid if they move from the doors, they may get stuck on the train.

To all those non-commuter travellers who make my journey so entertaining- why would anyone take the opportunity to travel at peak time unless they absolutely have to? Please, it is like it is part of the tourist holiday trip 'Take the London Underground when it is peak travel time' Is it on your tour itinerary to ram yourself on to the packed train just for fun to say 'Wow my trip to London was great. I got to go on the London Underground and I got to ram myself on from a standing dive'. You jump into the crowd from a great height hoping there will be some space, even if you are in that last bit of space between the heads of everyone and the roof and laughing say 'I am coming in'. This is amazing fun; I can go back home and tell everyone how many people they squash into one underground carriage and how they melt everyone with the heat because there is no air-conditioning.

There are the tourists who make comments about using a cattle prod to push everyone in further and seem to think 'Oh I am getting off and I think it would be amazing fun to just push everyone off'

Then there are the tourists who have been shopping on Oxford Street who also bring a long a whole shopping trolley of boots shoes clothes and carrying a coffee with a sandwich and then proceeds to get on after their bags because they do not want to leave them with everyone on the platform.

There are also tourists who get on before their zillion shopping bags with everyone on the platform pushing their bags on after them, whilst we all watch the doors shut, then open, then shut, then open at which point everyone on the carriage all heave to get those zillion shopping bags on the train just so we can get to our journeys next destination.

The Desperate

To all the people who appear with prams, suitcases, babies, children, at PEAK travel time: I mean seriously, do you know how annoying this is to all of the seasoned commuters? Have you watched their faces? Have you seen the look of 'Oh Jeez, what are you doing here'? You completely disrupt our entire existence in our (note OUR) environment. You clog up the exits, the entrance, ticket halls, and payment machines because you don't have a clue on its function. You stop and dither as though the rest of us have all the time in the world to wait for you to decide which way is what. You also differ about what train you are going to get on; personally I just find you a challenge and all that tweaking my plan of attack strategy is good for keeping the brain in tip top condition. There are occasions when I think 'Are you mad?' Who would travel peak CRUSH hour with a pram the size of a bus and who would inflict it on their beloved children? Or not so beloved? And why would you give the said toddler an ice cream or a burger and chips? (Yes, I have seen both; those sticky fingers; that sticky wet floor; that poor man's trousers!)

The Stinkers

To the stinkers, I mean seriously, do you think it's acceptable to stink the carriage out with your BO (bodily odour – to those who are unfamiliar) and make everyone feel faint because they have had to stop breathing - it's that or throw up? Do you think these stinkers have no sense of smell? Because surely if they did, they would also be going green with everyone else. And how can they smell so bad first thing in the morning? Why not just give us all a break and have a shower?

Some people prefer to stay in bed that extra hour, (or more), and then roll out and onto the train fully dressed (if we are lucky) all without undertaking the normal daily rituals the rest of us like to undertake, like; going via the shower, teeth cleaning or at least a swill of the mouth wash. Trust me, we all know who you are as soon as you enter the great world of the London Underground and it is compounded when you then enter the underground carriage (and this applies to both sexes!). PLEASE GIVE IS US ALL A BREAK and be late for work or get out of bed earlier, we would all rather you did because, seriously, we do not appreciate the aroma, smell, stink, or odours emitting from you.

Thank you to that amazing smelly person who sat close (thankful not right next to me) how on earth do you manage to get to smell like that? Oh and those feet; I have never seen such ugly (even on a man) or dirty feet in a pair of wonderful sandals (seriously should men be allowed to wear sandals?)

The Seat Giver

Thank you to the delightful young lad who gave me his seat and just jumped on to his Dad's lap and said he was happy to give his seat up for me because his Dad's lap was more comfortable.

The Sleepers

To the man sat next to me who fell fast asleep and woke with a start and a jump; confused and disoriented he said 'sorry' to me because obviously he thought he had been asleep in my lap! He hadn't but I accepted his apology because I didn't want him to get even more confused when I explained that it was his own lap and not mine, so I just smiled and said 'no worries'.....He then promptly fell asleep again.

Oh the times of becoming extra friendly with all those people who fall asleep on what is clearly my shoulder. I think of the onetime where the chap was just far too young, I really was not looking for a toy boy in his early twenties and everyone thinking I clearly was with him. There is only so much hair gel that is acceptable to have transferred on to ones clothes by a sleeping stranger who I really just want to push either on to some other persons shoulder or on the floor!! But I just politely, and somewhat gingerly, prod them with my elbow in order to attract enough of their attention just to remind them where they are and that you are not their comfort cushion, or even someone who they can snuggle up too. After the third attempt of reminding the said sleeper, you either ignore them hoping he will get off eventually, or you push him off with such force they ricochet off the sides of the carriage and end up 3 miles up the carriage in a heap but very awake!!

The Sharers

I now know every message tone and every ring tone that a smart phone can emanate. I have also listened to a number of music albums I would never have normally listened too because the person down the carriage obviously wanted everyone to listen to his personal music; Are they aiming to be deaf? Or, do they just like sharing their taste in music?

The Baby

Thank you for preparing me for sudden motherhood without even noticing it; whilst undertaking the usual 'oh my god I have to get on that train no matter what', my tunnel vision switched on to its fullest extent with no visionary senses to see that baby reaching out to clutch your backpack just has you make that leap onto the carriage. The baby just thinks it's taken flight and squeals in delight has it shoots out of its mother's arms and joins me on the train. Nobody utters a word because everyone is indifferent to the fact, I have suddenly gained a baby that does not belong to me, most will not even have noticed as they are so blinkered or plugged into their devices.

Even I am still oblivious until I spot a seat and try to seat down. As soon as I hear this muffled sound, I of course then remove my backpack and there it was! I mean where did that come from? What am I supposed to do with it now? It peers up with big blue eyes and giggles at me like I am the best thing that has ever happened to it. So, after some serious tickling I alight at the next stop and hand it in to lost property saying that I found it on the underground.

Health Warning

WARNING; No matter how hungry you are, DO NOT, I repeat DO NOT eat anything from your bare hands after your commute because those zillions of creatures attached to those handrails will soon be in your mouth swelling around on that sandwich you have just chucked in there. Using COMMUTER INFECTED hands to eat from is just a, NO, just think about all of those hands that exited the toilet with no soap or water touching them, those hands that have been up someone's nose, those hands that have been licked or sucked on and those same hands have attached themselves to that same handrail your hand has hung on to before you then unwrapped that poor defenceless sandwich which you have now just infected with a zillion bugs

The Fashionista's

Thank you everyone for the large and very varied fashion parade on the underground; I have no need to attend any London Paris Milan fashion week, just get on the underground and see a daily fashion parade for free. The good, bad, and the ugly, every Monday to Friday. Let's take the lady dressed in black apart from those vivid red shoes, awesome idea lady, a little flash of colour. Then there are the guys who have their trousers around their knees and their Calvin's showing not so cool, in fact you hold the commuter herd up because your stride is reduced to baby steps, there are also the men in dapper suits, waist coats and tie; you look awesome. The constant brain chatter, 'wow I love those shoes', 'that skirt is so wrong!', 'I like that jacket', 'nice bag', 'great watch', 'oh my god that's just so WRONG' is exhausting

Sunglasses are always an interesting thing to wear on the underground. The wearers obviously do not realise that there isn't any sunshine down in the underground and as soon as they hit the depths of the underground, they can't see a thing. Amusingly they point blankly refuse to take them off because obviously wearing sunglasses on the underground looks just so bang on trend. Never mind they won't be able to see because the sun doesn't shine down there, commuters wear dull black clothes, so the wearer of the sun glasses will be bouncing off everyone, tripping over the steps, falling into the carriages, not seeing that crevasse between platform and carriage and head butting the doors because they will not have realised they are shut!

Every single day on London underground is London fashion week. If you love people watching then the world of the underground is a kaleidoscope of colours (well actually black mostly but then when you do get the odd bright colour you are shocked out of the commuter trance like you have just been smacked round the head) there are long skirts; dangerous for running up and down the stairs ladies and gentleman if you prefer a skirt; seriously do not wear a long flowing skirt with an elastic waist band because trust me this will lead to some embarrassment has the person directly behind you running down those same stairs to get that train that has just pulled into the station is going to step on that skirt and has you continue on your way it will either ping you back into standing position if the elastic is industrial strength or your skirt will just pull down and expose you pants if you remembered to put some on in your rush to get of the door that morning and we all know they will be the oldest pair you own!, Or you expose your bottom cheeks in that G-string or if you forgot to put any on you will just be exposed and everyone coming up behind will be stunned into silence! Or will break out in applause! You on the other hand will try and regain any modest with the fleet of a hand without looking back like it never happened; that's of course if standing on your skirt you did not then fall forward the skirt still under the foot of the stranger who then leaves you face down with your derrière exposed to the massive of people bringing up your rear (pardon the pun) has they step over you

Story Telling

Thank you for enabling me to have the opportunity to make up someone's entire life story all within the space of my commute its great; You look at someone and plan out their entire life plan without even uttering one single word to them. For example the young couple travelling to work; the two that have the pleasure of travelling together, they get a seat next to each other on the start of their commute with their brief cases business suits and newspaper looking like it's a life time's achievement because they are so grown up and have joined the rat race of that great commuting brigade. The great adventure (it will soon fade into a pale, 'I am so exhausted and sick of all of this WHY AM I DOING THIS DAY IN DAY OUT!!') they sit there arm in arm and you steal a look and suddenly build up a picture of their life story just by how they are dressed and act with each other. So here is one I did earlier they would be married within the next 2 years having may be got that small pay rise and after a holiday or two they will then proceed into that marital bliss, still on the commute (you can tell the longer term married couples because they will get on separate carriages or if they get on the same carriage will barely acknowledge each other let alone sit together). The newlyweds will then have mapped out the 2.5 kids larger house and family car on the drive mow the lawn on Saturdays and wash the car on Sunday. The husband will continue with that daily commute, whilst they put the kids through university then he will retire, so exhausted from the commuting that he will spend the rest of his days on the golf course unless he managed to buy that villa in Spain.

On the other hand that couple who dress and acted so conservatively, may be extreme adrenalin junkies just back from snowboarding or jumping off a mountain..... I doubt it though their hair was too trim and neat

The entertainment

To the two young lads who got on the deathly quiet carriage on the morning run before 8am; it was interesting to watch everyone's reaction when you started to show each other some music clips; (which weren't too loud I hasten to add). People started to look around to see who dared, yes, how someone dare have the cheek to make some noise before 8am especially some music. Once they register that the noise is coming from you, they fix you with a raised eyebrow and an evil stare (in the hope that it may turn you to stone). Even the guy opposite woke up from his half sleep to see who dared have the cheek to make some noise. You both carried on oblivious to everyone's annoyance.

The lost

Thank you to the train driver who explained they were holding teddy for collection because they found him sat terrified on the carriage barely able to utter a word because his friend of 5 years old, had left him as he rushed off the train and before Teddy could leap up after him, the doors had shut. Poor Teddy was left peeled to the window screaming after his friend, 'you have forgotten me HELP ME STOP TURN ROUND PLEASE!'

Sinking Heart

That sinking heart feeling of 'I am NEVER going to get home' (funny how you do not get the same reaction when going to the office) when you arrive at your platform after speed walking the distance between alighting one underground line taking all known short cuts to get to your next platform in your allotted time frame of 2 milliseconds; you know that target you set yourself daily and you just want to always better your best time so you devise even better route plans taking the stairs (down because we all know taking the stairs up requires herculean strength and commitment even to get to the first base) two or three at a time and if they are spiral steps you take the narrowest steps on the inner spiral just to cut that half a second off your time, all whilst knowing the risks are great in terms of injury (basically breaking your neck though the embarrassment hurts more) you then alight mid-air at a gallop so you land further from the bottom step (ladies do not try this in heels it's far too dangerous) you crash land with a thud but you are two metres further down than normal so there is your 2 seconds off your best time. You stride forward not looking at the surge of people coming towards you because it is all about commitment to your chosen path and your strength of conviction. THEY WILL move out of the way first......surely, they will? So you lose precision time as you dart into a gap between the crowd who are going in the same direction (a more full proof plan is to get right behind some big six foot guy who looks terrifying to anyone coming towards him but for you it's like having a speeding juggernaut in front to shield off any attempts to slow you down. You obviously have to make sure this person is travelling at breakneck speed (speed of light is better) which creates a back draft around you, so you exert less energy.

In fact, to save energy, and because the likelihood of him noticing is zero, just climb aboard his back pack and hitch a lift to conserve energy.

Bang you have made it to your next platform, BOOM it hits you, its rammed 10 deep and your heart, though joyous in beating your record time, now sinks to your feet because there is no way you are getting on your next train for at least 3 hours. So, you just slump deflated in a heap on the floor.

New Friends

Thank you for enabling me to make friends outside of my 1 zillion friends on social media. I have made friends with many people whilst travelling on the London Underground, you know the ones you see day in day out who get on the same carriage as you and sit on the same seat or those waiting in the same place on the platform. You see these people more than you family husband or wife. The ones that you give a silent nod of acknowledgement to but would rarely if ever actually say 'good morning' to because that's not commuter cool! Oh no, you can't break that silence and just say 'Hi have a nice day or here we are again' because you are too afraid that person may strike up a conversation which continues your entire journey. That would never do because you would then become one of those 'different' people or god forbid become a human who talks on the train and that just wouldn't do your commuter cred any good would it? And the entire carriage would be quietly listening to your conversation like it was a radio show or silently telling you to SHUT UP!

Lost Shoe

I can now get a lost shoe back on the foot in the blink of an eye when some person behind is getting off the train quicker than me or plainly did not notice that in this instance there was actually a person directly in front of them. In fact, I am surprised they did not notice because they had me squashed up against the door, meaning I was propelled out once the carriage door opened, and in the process they took my shoe off. So whilst still stuck to the person behind I managed to stealthy bend with outstretched hand, locate the lost shoe and place back on my foot without losing the traction that ensured I was still in front of the person who was behind. Without any effort I managed to get airlifted all the way to the escalator at which point I asked the person who was directly behind if they could put me down!

All seasoned commuters know not to stop and bend down in slow tourist fashion to pick up that lost shoe because we know that we will be knocked over by the galloping herd behind us. Because the galloping herd of commuters are on a mission to get to work, or that coffee shop precisely one nanosecond before their previous best from yesterday. If you had been delirious enough to collect the lost shoe you would have being peeling yourself off the germ infested platform floor said shoe in hand covered in the shoe prints of a thousand people who never noticed you bend down.

Temperature Control

Note there are only two fabulous temperatures available on the London Underground, sub-zero in the winter months and above boiling in the summer; let no one fool you it's one or the other. The only good thing is it does not rain on the underground!

I can quietly undertake a controlled sweat without anyone noticing. Sometimes however, I feel so hot that I really do not care that I am sweating buckets in that metal can with hundreds of other sweaty bodies so I whip out a tissue, or cloth and dab in a lady like manner, or just wipe because I have lost all sense of decorum at this point. Usually at this point I feel as though I am beginning to melt like the witch in the Wizard of OZ (and I know you have all watched the Wizard of OZ and know the scene I am referring to, so don't pretend you don't) because it's like a running river, I am quietly screaming 'I am melting I am melting'. Strangely have you noticed the more you concentrate on your melting the more you sweat?! Relief doesn't come until the doors open and you shoot out like you've have just popped out of the tube at the water park.

Oh the wonderful heat in the summer, those blissful
sunny hot days which turn into sweltering HOT, I am going
to die and become a pool of SWEAT on the underground;
when you are sat there, profusely trying to control not
melting or looking like you have just emerged from a
swimming pool (at the time you wish you had) on a 1000
degree humid underground carriage with all those heated
bodies in the same carriage up close. You sit up straight
breath deep and meditate with your eyes shut ....this
basically means telling yourself it is not full of hot sweating
bodies in a carriage that has no cool air coming anywhere
near you and you keep telling yourself I am not sweating I
AM NOT SWEATING, my face is not running with sweat, it
is not dripping down my neck until you have quietly talked
yourself out of sweating (this is because you have none left
to give or everyone has got off the train and the doors are

left open!!). This tactic is only flawed when suddenly a lady sits next to you, not just any lady but one of those delightful people who as soon as they are in front of a seat they start to sit and then have no control. It's as if just after SIT has reached their brain, gravity takes them full pelt to whatever is about to receive their derriere. I am surprised this lady did not go straight through the carriage floor taking the seat with her but thankfully it held. This small triumph is immediately outweighed by the fact that this lady has now not only occupied her own seat but is also occupying a large proportion of my seat too. I am sharing my seat with said lady along with the seat she is sat on. I am pinned down by her shoulder and arm because there is no room for all of her body parts on the seat she has chosen. I am just thankful she didn't choose to sit in my seat or misjudge her seating plan. I carry on with my 'do not sweat/ I am not boiling' meditation and the strange thing was the shoulder and arm, that was impeding any attempt on my behalf of escape was cool like the lady had just come out of an ice box. I grappled with telling her to unpin me or continue to feel and take the coolness of the shoulder and arm to cool me down (either that or just slap her for her rudeness expecting two seats and her constant movement of said shoulder and arm what a fidget). I decided to take the course of temperature control to reduce my overheated one in the hope that she was going to get off before me otherwise I would have to start extracting myself from her cover about 10 minutes before my stop, whilst underneath the arm and shoulder hoping not to slip further underneath the shoulder and arm and ending up lost forever. The lady thankfully gets out of her seat to exit the carriage the stop before I am due to a light – HALLELUJAH!

I love the summer months with the warm light evenings, the gardens full of blooming flowers, that wonderful smell of cut grass, the sound of the lawn mower and outside dining with everyone smiling. Then you enter the underground; the sweaty, hot and stifling underground the carriage that's only airflow are the windows at each end of the carriages. That is if someone has had the sense to open them because they themselves have reached a temperature of 1000 degrees. However, there is always that person who hasn't opened the window because their hair will get ruined with the hot stifling air that will be released as soon as the window is dropped down. The rest of the carriage will be sat cursing the moron for not opening the window; unless of course someone has shouted 'OPEN that blasted window you idiot your hair will be fine and we don't care about the boiling hot air and soot that is about to be released just OPEN IT NOW!

The moron will oblige because they will not want to refuse such a direct polite request to do so in front of everyone who then turns to look at them. What can they say to embarrass themselves further, No? 'It will ruin my hair?' 'I don't know how to' when it clearly tells you how to (trust me, you will figure it out in two seconds!) Once the moron politely concedes with a smile and drops the window everyone suddenly relaxes.

The best place to stand is in the middle of the seats nearest to the front carriage window, here you can catch the HOT breeze (it just circulates the hot air) or just stay rammed up against the doors and windows which seems to be the favoured position of most because they are all worried they may not be able to exit at their stop.

Thank you to the two rather large men who on a sub-zero freezing winters day offered the only heating on the underground carriage that day (is there any heating on the London Underground?). The only seat available was between you both and I snuggled down into that seat and had central heating my entire journey. The body heat from you both was like being wrapped in a heated blanket, absolute bliss.

Virus Carrier

Oh that sinking feeling when someone sneezes next to you, this normally occurs, when you finally manage to secure a seat (through a determined stare or two) and then within a few minutes the person you have sat down next to lets go of all effort or decorum to show everyone within 20 paces they have some disease, which they are so happy to share; as they let go of 50 loud infectious sneezes in under 2 seconds then reach into their bag for a snot soaked hankie. They then proceed to wipe their snivelling very red nose on the germ-infested cloth that is of course, if you have sat next to someone who has the common decency to actually use a tissue or hankie. Sadly we all know that is not always the case and instead they will heave that snot straight back up their nose (I have yet to see someone yuk it out on a underground carriage, so thank god for small mercies). Throughout this episode you are thinking to yourself 'oh for god sake you are infecting me with whatever disease you have up that nose!' 'Oh god I am now going to be in bed ill, for the next 6 weeks, starting from tonight!!' 'I really just can't afford to take the time off work......' 'if you infect me I will just have to be a disease carrier and pretend I am perfectly fine', for us women this means being a bit heavier on the make-up and hope your nose only runs between your platform marathons and you don't breath the entire time you are in the train underground carriage (you of course faint but which is more embarrassing ?; snot infestation carrier and everyone knowing and trying to move as far away as possible or fainting through not breathing ?. Surely, it is obvious that fainting wins and anyway if you faint you will never fall over because there is nowhere to fall, all those hundreds of bodies will keep you up right and then you will wake up eventually still in the same position and bingo, no snot. Or god forbid, you may even get offered a seat!

People Watching

On a daily basis I get to do my favourite pastime, people watching; I mean seriously where else can you sit (or standing generally!) And watch so many people in the space of an hour's commute but on the London Underground? It's such a mixture of people, clothes, styles and people going about their daily business. Though some people share far too much because they still think they are in their front room! I get to understand the latest styles; men and beards seems to have been a trend that continues to grow (pardon the pun), black is certainly the colour of the entire 21st century for the commuter by far, but hey what idiot would choose to wear white (which we all know would have turned grey if you are lucky, black if you are not by the end of the day !) Then there are the trainers versus stylish flat shoes, and I know which I would choose trainers are so 90s yuppie darling! However ultimately more sensible so I concur. The cap that just sits on top of the head back to front is one style I have never understood

I mean why wear one and it makes the head twice as big as it actually is or maybe that's the point because the person wearing it has tiny head? Then the pants and trousers down to your knees always makes me smile when they are struggling to walk so end up doing little baby steps because that is so much more cool than pulling your trousers up! Seriously it isn't, even a toddler would have walked pass you in your effort to look cool

The drinkers

Oh my god I raise my glass (or bottle in this case) to the people, who pre-9am, can drink vodka straight from the bottle; those three builders from our close EU neighbouring countries (how do I know they were builders? Well because they also bought along enough drills, buckets and shovels to build the Shard!!). I mean seriously, how on earth do you open a bottle of vodka and proceed to drink it at that time of the morning, I cannot even look at a cake without thinking 'oh god far too early for me' the vodka would have had me retching. The best bit was watching the reaction in the carriage you instantly put everyone on the defensive thinking 'don't be causing any trouble on here', with half the men thinking 'oh god don't cause any trouble', because I may have to make the decision of 'do I a). Stop reading my paper?' 'b). Do I need to pretend I have not noticed anything?', 'c). Do I have to try and look so small no one will notice and what happens if they see me and say something?' or 'd). Do I have to stand up and man up, maybe I will become a hero?' ('Is there enough room for me to stand up?') Then you see their demeanour change as they debate 'well if there is any trouble there are enough people to help me if I get stuck or will they just carry on reading their phones, paper, book pretending nothing is happening'. At this point the builders are getting a bit loud (god I hope they are not on their way to work otherwise it will become the house that jack built with a slight lean to the right!) and everyone is trying to ignore them and trying to move slightly away, (but of course there isn't any space to move to); Then all of a sudden they alight the carriage and are gone. I watch the aforementioned debating men as they instantly feel a huge sense of relief and the underground carriage returns back to the nothingness

I mean seriously can you actually drink neat vodka that early in the morning without gagging? And not miss your stop because you end up asleep going around and around the underground time and again until you realise its noon and you had been on your way to work.

/ou for teaching me how to play mind
/ith myself as an alternative to learning
,nguages such as, Spanish Chinese and
r   .tually would help me to listen to others
conve,   ,oing on in my underground carriage but
instead I se. how long I can gaze out of the window on the
carriage before someone blocks my view, which is about
five seconds! This all occurs before the train hits the
underground or in the winter's darkness when all you can
see is a reflection of yourself looking fresh, and fabulous,
especially first thing in the morning. Ha! If only! It's more
likely to be the look, you know the one where you are still
deathly white and in your pyjamas, (unless you were lucky
enough to remember to change your clothes before you left
the house), that you see looking back at you.

Have you noticed how the reflections on the doors show
people who are stood near them with four legs - two in their
usual position and then two on their head?

Amazing what you notice on the London Underground, obviously this can only be seen from a sitting position and when you are not compacted all together like sardines in a tin.

I love the fact I will never have the urge to go amongst the funny mirrors you get at the seaside because I can do this every weekday on the train. I can make my head three times the size it is through the windows of the carriage which are directly opposite me. Then by changing angle and position you can make yourself look normal (which is fairly difficult at that time of the morning when only a bucket of coffee will make you fully functional and presentable) or you can completely distort you face and head so you look like a you have a tefal head with an extraordinarily large forehead. Have you noticed how bald heads end up looking like one amazingly large egg?

Those Conversations

I now have such an amazing insight into other people's lives due to the fact people seem to believe that a conversation held within the confines of the underground carriage is entirely private; an example, in the space of ten minutes I became a dear friend, full of knowledge of a stranger sat next to me between two stations. I knew where he was living (Devon and due to his wife getting a job in London the family had to move to Uxbridge), he had a British passport (though not from the UK originally but he had married an English lady from Birmingham), he had children of a young age and therefore he needed to earn plenty of money to provide for them (I gather he was on a recruitment call and yes he did actually say that and I thought 'don't we all darling'), he apparently had lots of experience (though he never said what in), he wanted a salary of £100,000 (though he had not said why he deserved this apart from he needed to support his family), and he was available in 2 weeks. I quietly got off the train at this point otherwise I may have ended up with his national insurance number, and his shoe size!

Suitable Attire

I view every purchase of clothing or shoes with a commuter head; will this be suitable for the underground? Will it show too much flesh if I sit down? Will I actually be able to sit down in it? Will it raise up has I reach up for the ceiling hand rails which most people struggle to reach? Will it blow up as I descend down the escalators, or show my knickers for all to see when I ascend up the escalators? Will it catch on someone's bag or clothing?, (this is lethal when they are exiting because you or your clothing will end up going with them!) Will it catch as you exit the carriage, on the bag which is pegged down by a twenty stone male pinging you back into the carriage like you are on a piece of elastic. The male whose bag it is doesn't notice you are now attached to him and his back pack when he exits at the next station. You of course are acting as if nothing is happening and everything is normal because you do not want to draw attention to yourself as you travel up the escalator with your legs dangling until you quietly manage to release yourself before the male mule exits the station.

Oh the numerous times I have seen the disasters of unsuitable clothing on the underground!

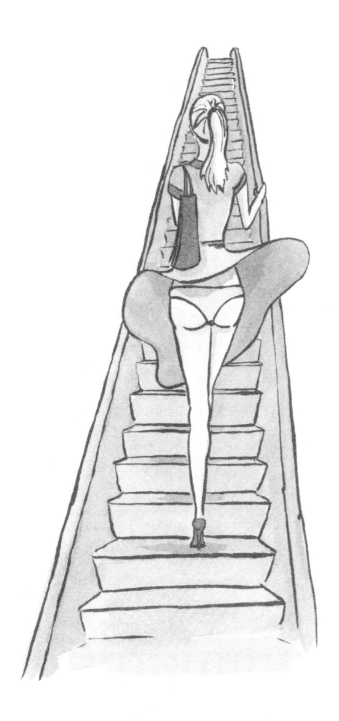

The Rule Breakers

To all the slow people, who instead of standing over to the right, always ALWAYS stand in the middle to block all the commuter migration. We REALLY need them to stand on the right and stop getting in everyone's way because they either, do not know the unwritten rule of the underground or they do not care. It really is advisable to stick to the rules and get out of the way of the commuter herd otherwise you may find yourself propelled from the masses behind and end up plastered to the left wall. Leaving the station staff to peel you off the wall, so you can continue your slow, middle of the road walk.

The Snorer

Thank you for enabling me to listen, along with the rest of the carriage, to the very loud sound of a hydraulic drill, aka your snoring! I mean seriously, can that amount of noise come out of one man's mouth? His household must have to wear industrial ear plugs to shut that noise out! He must have been seriously tired or so drunk (there was no alcohol aroma so I don't believe it was an alcoholic induced pig snore) because why else would you inflict that noise on the carriage and embarrass yourself, or maybe he thought he was at home sat on the sofa in front of the TV? I had the pleasure of occupying the position just in front of him where he was slumbered in the seat with his head back (most people fall on their own lap, someone else's lap or shoulder, this is the first time I had seen someone asleep in this position on an underground carriage) and oh the noise that was coming out of that mouth! I really had no idea one individual person had the capacity to make such a deafening noise. I am astonished he did not wake himself up but clearly not because I looked straight into his gaping mouth which was like looking down the Blackwall Tunnel. I did debate whether I should move away from the danger zone because with a mouth that size, I may actually fall in! Maybe if I fell in it would wake him up? and block the noise coming out of it (which I am sure would be a relief to everyone within a mile of him) at which point the train did an emergency stop (you know the kind. The driver then says 'move away from the doors! Move away from the doors!') It jolts the mouth shut, the head comes up the eyes open he sits up and pretends that he has been reading the book in his lap and not just given the entire carriage a lesson on how not to fall asleep on the London Underground!!

I seriously did not know you could be stood up and fall asleep with your mouth open first thing in the morning on a moving tin can. Well I get it's a Monday and maybe you had a tough weekend but seriously you must be knackered to be able to stand there asleep with your mouth open, catching flies, and then when you do open your eyes because the train jolts, you clearly have no idea where you are. You simply tuck your arm around the hand rail and tuck you head in the corner of the carriage door (let's hope he does not fall out when the doors open because there is not quite enough rammed bodies in the carriage to hold him up just yet) It is very clear this man has had one hell of a weekend by the looks of things. Maybe he would have been better staying at home because he will find himself at work wondering how the hell he got there or he will be in this carriage dribbling down the door window as he slumbers against it with his mouth firmly stuck to the window and of course when the doors open he will just slide left and right with the door. Maybe I should just get up and slap him?

Yellow Line

There is absolutely no smartness about waiting the wrong side of the yellow line and if the driver tells you off when you get on the carriage 'to the person who was not stood behind the yellow line I was not waving at you to say 'hello!', the yellow line is for your own safety' you very seriously must have REALLY been over the yellow line! The driver should have given out a full description of you so we could all look at you like the stupid moron that you are. You would not have got on the train any quicker unless you wanted to be on the front of the train where there are clearly no seats!

The Boogie Alert (and I am not talking about golf!)

It is always shocking how many people like to chase boogies up their nose whilst in the company of others! I mean seriously do you have to? It is so repulsive how they always have to check to see if they have managed to actually catch one on their finger and, if they have not managed to catch one, they then go up for another go like it's some competition. They keep going until they have managed to find one and hook it on the end of their finger. YUK! They clearly don't realise that some of us have just had breakfast.

The worse bit is when they then think 'shit now what do I do with it'? And look around to see what they can attach it too, which will invariably be some part of the carriage furnishings!! Now, I know people pick their noses, but most decent people do this with a tissue and whilst in the privacy of their own home. Seriously, we do not care how you organise the inside of your nose whilst in the privacy of your own home, or where the droppings go, but DO NOT DO THIS ON THE UNDERGROUND CARRIAGE PLEASE!

Thank you to the lady (well now that would need to be redefined after my next statement!) whilst I was waiting on the platform, the underground carriage pulled up, doors opened to reveal you stood there with your finger stuck so far up your nose that I am surprised it wasn't poking out of your eye! I had just had breakfast you obviously had not! You just carried on like you were in your own front room. I am sure my face displayed at first amazement, then shock when you made no effort to remove your finger from up your nose (maybe it had lodged itself up there and you were struggling to remove it?) You then glanced at me and merrily carried on looking for your breakfast! I mean seriously why did you not remain at home and cook yourself something to eat instead of rummaging around up your nose? Or couldn't you at least of waited until you were at your desk, or in the toilet. I really feel like it should be a criminal offense to clear out your nose on public transport! It's not just the picking and disposing of the findings you inflict on us, there is also the matter of your sticky fingers (assuming you managed to find something up there), all over the handrails for the rest of us to pick up the debris from your nose. I therefore stepped up and around you and made my way to the far end of that carriage just to ensure any unconsumed sticky green things, which you had left in the area, did not attach themselves to me or my clothing.

Another day another nose picker; RIGHT NEXT TO ME! WHY ME, OH WHY ME! I wish the guy next to me would stop messing around up his nose and then checking his fingers to see if his fishing trip up his nose had been successful. He obviously did this so naturally in his front room that he forgot he was on a crowded train or maybe this is where he always undertook a nose fishing trip because he had some spare time; I mean seriously go fishing in your own time and space and not when I am sat next to you quietly trying to read. You obviously didn't think I had noticed that you were going up your nose every five minutes and then checking to see if you had caught anything. When your fishing trip was successfully you then slyly dropped your hand down between us, flicking your catch on the floor! A sideways glance from me and a slight move away in the opposite direction to you, cut short your fishing expedition when you realised, I had seen all your fishing attempts. YOU DISGUSTING CREATURE!

I really have an adverse reaction of revulsion to any commuter who believes it is acceptable to dispose of their nose waste on the chair they happened to be sitting on! I really would never ever visit the person's house because surely their entire furniture must be encased in crustaceans of hard nose residue? Because they so naturally undertake the disposal of their nose residue whilst on the London Underground

This has been in evidence on many occasions and this time the man, young and dressed very smartly was sat opposite me on a packed carriage. Sadly I had finished every section of the paper and all my phone messages so I could either fall asleep and end up between someone's bottom cheeks or look across to see what was happening between the crushed bodies to the seat opposite.

The man sat on that seat was trying to dispose of his nose residue which was stuck like super glue to his finger

It was disgustingly fascinating watching him again and again trying to wipe this thing steadfastly clinging to his finger (rightly so because it did belong to him!!) on the bit of seat between his legs. He obviously did not care the next person to sit on the seat he would eventually vacate, would gain a cling on and when that person noticed this green hard bit attached to their clothing would try to pick it off not realising that it was a dried green boogie from someone else's nose!!

Again and again he wiped his finger one way then the next then his whole hand, then the finger his boogie was stuck to backwards and forwards backwards and forwards each time checking his finger to see if the cling on was still there and he would start again and again getting more desperate until finally his finger was clear and there it was as large as life stuck to the seat waiting for the poor soul who would pick it up as soon as they sat down!!

The Virus Alert

Okay everyone the virus alert; we all know and dread that someone in the carriage who is happy to spread their germs all around. We all try to steer clear of sitting/standing near them or try holding our breath so as not to breathe in those dreaded germs when that person is coughing, snorting and sneezing. Even though the sharer makes a mild attempt to catch those flying particles which have just shot from both mouth and nose, the germs are generally caught by the people directly opposite. You can attempt to deflect them by using your bag to defend yourself but it's like a game of tennis, you defend and chuck it back across to the offending opponent, who just as quickly sends another one across. Fortunately, to your left a person has swiftly extracted a can of antiseptic spray and aims it like a gun directly at the offending opponent, before burying them entirely in a foam like film of sweet-smelling antiseptic. After a successful delivery they just as quickly drop the spray back into their bag and return to their reading. What a hero!

The pusher inner

There is always a slight joyous moment when denying someone the pleasure of trying to gain entry to the carriage when they are so clearly behind you but have the audacity to push passed through the very slight gap on the inside, just as you try to enter the carriage. In their haste and rudeness, they had forgotten they also had a rather large bag attached to their shoulder which had remained behind them (because it had more manners than its owner). On realising this you triumph as you close the entire gap stopping the bag following its audacious owner. You pause to let the pusher realise they are stuck; however they are refusing to look back knowing you may give them a slap for their utter rudeness. They continue to try and enter the carriage on what is now a piece of elastic, so you just hang tough for a enough seconds to let them know they cannot go any further no matter how hard they try, until you relinquish their bag.

On their final heave-ho you step onto the carriage releasing the bag just at the same moment with perfect timing. The bag front loads so fast it smacks the impertinent idiot in the back of the head knocking them straight to the floor; you of course just step over them smiling in delight. Oh the satisfaction!

One for the Ladies

Oh ladies, some of those makeup bags are huge; seriously I would rather go without the war paint than carry that around with me all day! Some look like the makeup counters you see in the shops. The largest ever bag was pulled from a rucksack that looked like it had the kitchen sink in it; she pulled that thing out and set it up across the empty carriage and proceeded to inflict all that colour and dust across anyone within three yards of her! Flick, Flick, Flick, with that brush and off all that dust and face particles went across those empty seats and anyone sat within forty paces!

There is life above ground

I have to thank the underground for completely failing one morning, with not a single train arriving or departing; this one thing gave me the opportunity to exit the underground and walk the fifteen minutes to Borough High Street, something I would not normally have undertaken unless coerced to do so. Yes, I know most people would have hopped on a bus or taken a taxi. This opportunity however, allowed me to see the great city of London in all its glory (ok it did help that the sky was blue and you could feel the sun) and I walked across London Bridge to see such an amazing view of the Thames. Unfortunately, the amount of people passing me in the opposite direction was like a massive army of ants (though clothed). There were zillions of them all coming towards me! I was walking behind the single sparse line of people going across the bridge towards London Bridge. I am sure if the mighty had fallen in their path they would have ended up stuck to the pavement as the relentless army of ants matched on not noticing the fallen. I choose to walk on the opposite side of the bridge after that experience.

Passenger arrangement

To the wonderful man who lifted, pushed and shoved me onto that rammed carriage; I had no intention of getting on because it was too rammed but thanks anyway because you managed to cram me into a space which did not exist, when the carriage doors opened. By some miracle you managed to make enough space for us both so well done, clearly you were going to get on that carriage even if the platform was 10 deep and you were at the back. With your superhuman strength we would have all been on it rammed into every space possible, even the head space which no one seems to have quite got the hang of climbing in to. You would be such a star in Japan, a champion, where they have passenger arrangement staff to push people onto packed trains during rush hour! You would be a King people pusher. Why pay for passenger arrangement staff when people like you who do it for free on London Underground?

One for the Cleaners

Thank you to all the cleaners who pick up after us all; all that rubbish we leave behind because many are just too lazy to take it off the trains and deposit it in the appropriate rubbish containers. These sloths are too self-absorbed to offer up a 'good morning/day/evening' to the cleaners they walk past day in day out. You cleaners do a sterling job, and if I catch your eye whilst going past, I will always wish you a 'good day'. So, thank you to the cleaners and sorry for all those people who do not see you. I don't think they do it intentionally it is just the commuter façade; as soon as they emerge from that great underground beneath the London streets they suddenly become human again. I will always try and remain human enough to offer pleasantries and you always do the same in return. On behalf of all commuters, you do a sterling job.

The Deluded

To the three VERY DELUDED women who decided one morning to join the commuter migration, at peak morning rush hour, with clearly no experience of London Underground or the task in hand. Each had a suitcase larger than an elephant; had you been away for a year?

They blocked the entire surge of commuter rush hour traffic at the exit. I mean please, why would you get to the bottom of those steps, stop and block the entire stair well whilst deciding how you were going to manoeuvre those HUGE trunk sized suitcases? Your incompetence had no effect in halting the mass coming from behind, it simply unblocked your blockage with such force that you and your cases ended up shooting out of that stair well to the path outside the station. I can picture you now, sat there on the path, wondering how you had got there; like a cork unloading from a shaken champagne bottle!

The Gobblers

Thank you to the man who thinks eating what appeared to be a breakfast (his eating habits were so diverse and quick, I really was not sure what was going in his mouth), it was utterly fascinating to watch; I felt compelled to watch, as though I was watching an animal at the zoo (and I am still trying to think of where I have seen an animal eat like this before, maybe a pig but I love pigs, so I really did not want to associate them with this person). It was just a fabulous way of showing how attractive you were has you rammed that food in your mouth and then proceeded to spit and drop it all over your suit, the seat and then the floor. It was amazing! I always thought the objective of eating was to keep it in one's mouth, not to spray anyone within a few feet with the contents,(luckily I, nor others, where sat within spitting distance) and to ensure it was chewed and swallowed with at least some decorum. Most people would make sure it went to their stomach, not the surrounding area. Then once the food had been disposed of whether in your mouth, across your attire, the surrounding seat, wall and flooring you then threw all of the wrappings on the floor to join the rest of the debris you had deposited.

To the young lady who got on the underground carriage at lunch time with some humongous, greasy, stinking what appeared to be a burger and then proceeded to devour the entire thing in one bite. I seriously did not think someone could eat that quickly. I did wonder if maybe she didn't want the stench to linger and that she was only thinking about her fellow commuters (some people are very thoughtful). However, when a burger is in a stifling hot underground carriage the smell is magnified somewhat, it will linger for weeks and seems to seep into your very being, so when you alight that pungent smell surrounds you like a halo of pong deep into your hair/clothes/bag. So then everyone thinks you have just eaten that smelly, greasy burger because obviously the only sign of it now (apart from the tell-tale wrapper, which she has kindly shoved down the side of the seat) is the smell coming from you.

The Red Face

To the man who made a senior professional board level grown up woman blush like a young girl because he choose to admire her coat, whilst on an absolutely packed to the ceiling London Underground carriage; In front of all those commuters minding their own business, in their own worlds, hoping no-one will single them out and they can quietly, and without any interruptions, go unnoticed but suddenly someone breaks rank and loudly decides to offer his admiration for a coat that was a bit different from the norm - green rather than the usual black. Commuters looked at him in disbelief at the fact that he had the audacity to do this through direct speech instead of through his own thoughts. Then everyone who heard, turned around to look at this item of such fascination, which caused a commuter to break that sacred silence and actually speak to a stranger - ME! How utterly embarrassing! Well the red heat that spread up my face was there for all to see! With shock I smiled and muttered my thanks wishing a big hole could swallow me up.

The Shirty

Sadly you also always get the commuters who after a little bit of standing around always gets a bit above themselves and a tad shirty (angry for those not familiar with the word shirty) because they are unable to deal with all the hot sweaty people travelling at peak time on the underground; When a carriage is rammed and you politely ask everyone to use all the available space that you can clearly see between the seats. The hot sweaty male in front (who obviously has had a bad day) seems to be unable to utter those words in front of everyone to help the people who are trying to board the train (some of who do not want to wait for the next train because the next train is not for another ten minutes!). You have no choice but to push his rather large bag due to the surge of people behind you who are controlling all your manoeuvring even with your brakes firmly on! He then says in a nice condescending way 'DO NOT push me', you look him directly in the eye (if you are rather tall – as I am – it is even more effective) and respond with 'I did not push you' as you are then squashed up against that rather large bag between the hot sweaty male (you feel like saying 'get a life, this is the rush hour mate'). He then follows this with another condensing 'DO NOT push me', at which point you are expecting him to follow that with an Incredible Hulk stance 'DON'T PUSH ME!' but there is not enough room because we are all squashed together. I look him in the eye and say with a smile 'feel free to get shirty if you want' followed by 'there is a surge of people behind me if you had not noticed so it is difficult to stop being manoeuvred straight into your rather large bag' then he says 'well why did you not say that in the first instance'. UMMMMMM now at this point you are thinking am I going to have to state the obvious? Whilst politely smiling at this moron Can you not see how rammed this carriage is? Are you from another planet? THIS IS PEAK RUSH HOUR ON THE LONDON UNDERGROUND, you do not get your own personal space and you will get poked, prodded, pushed, tripped, squashed, and trod on. If you do not like it then walk! You don't think I want to be pushed into another's body part or bag? I mean seriously, 'do any of us?'

Flip Flops

Now here is a sensible question for the thrill seekers or just plain stupid; why would you court danger by wearing flip flops, in the rush hour, on the London Underground? I mean, how on earth do people manage to keep them on let alone walk at any reasonable pace with them on? Most offices ban them because of those very reasons. Do they not get trapped in the escalators when exiting the stations or are they not a trip hazard for everyone else behind as you grapple with walking at any pace in them (that's why they are used on holiday because they encourage a slow chilled out pace and to stop the hot sand burning your feet! There is no sand on underground).

I know you want to show the sun has come out and you want to show your beautiful painted toe nails but seriously you are endangering all other commuters on their already great and hazardous journey through the underground. Why would you wish to be that one person to become a trip hazard? Do you not like your feet enough to want to protect them from those feet attached to a thirty stone weight descending down towards your flip-flopped foot? Do you not want to protect them from that trolley with those wheels that just happens to roll over your feet or anything else that is in its way because the owner really has no concern about your well-being, as long as that trolley is attached and following the same path they happened to have just squeezed through they will carry on like they are still a single entity. Do you not care as you catch your flip flop in the door as you exit the carriage?

And never mind your nail paint, it is a fine colour and don't those feet just look great.....you wait until the end of the day....you will have gone and bought some sensible shoes because those feet will be black and the vanish a lovely blue black colour that's if you have been lucky enough to retain your toe nails!

The Brave

Oh and the two old ladies who must have clocked up two hundred years between them. What a feat of achievement from Canary Wharf you navigated those amazing escalators that just seem to go on for ever - unless you managed to find the lifts. How well you managed to circumnavigate the underground and get to the platform through the thong of rush hour full of home goers. I applaud you both as you merrily held each other up in your gallant attempt of the underground environment in your extremely smart attire.

You both gingerly entered the packed carriage and I immediately offered up my seat, along with the stranger sat next to me, before you both fell over in a heap as the train started to depart. With my arms stretched out to catch your descent towards the floor, I ushered you into the now vacated seats (ok maybe I was being very presumptuous with the 'oh you can have both these seats' when I was sat only on one and gamely gave up the seat next to me, which at the time, was occupied by a stranger). Safely seated you settled yourself in like old (excuse the pun) pros that did this every day.

Oh pleasure and joy, we have a joyous person on the train not the usual miserable creature we all know as a commuter. Yes, someone, who is glad to be on the underground carriage and just for the sheer pleasure and joy of doing so, is strumming (and doing so very well) his guitar regardless of what anyone was thinking, unafraid of bringing attention to himself (and his very tight, short, red trousers) soft, smoothing music just lulled us all into another mode. He created Instant calm and happiness for a moment and then he got off and the carriage went back to normal

The Olympian

You will need herculean efforts of speed and agility to circumnavigate everything that will be in your path as soon as you descend beneath the streets of London. Your senses need to be tip top, your view 360 degrees and it also helps if you are awake at the same time! The agility of one's self is of high grade Olympian style; you can avoid emergency braking by others, stop and go round obstacles in nanoseconds, avoid that bag/ hand/foot/shoe/pram/dog/ toolbox/cat/budgie, hurdle over objects which randomly appear being dragged by someone in front with no thought of the trail of destruction left in their wake.

Then there is always the idiot who is so engrossed in their phone that their sense of direction has completely gone and their navigation switched off so they don't see the trolley (dog/cat/child/budgie), flip up in the air like a large skittle and on their descent, take out twenty people (which you stealthily avoid with an emergency brake and a swerve and then follow the clown with the trolley who is completely oblivious to the carnage behind them as they exit the underground).

The Crew

Thank you to the train drivers; we all appreciate you driving us to work and always enjoy any conversation you bestow on us commuters outside of the usual many announcements of:-

'Please mind the doors'

'This train is ready to depart mind the doors mind the doors'

'Please do not obstruct the doors'

'Please note, we will not stop at the next station'

'Please note, we are held at a red signal'

'Please note, we will be held here whilst we change drivers'

'Get away from the doors'

'Use all available space' (translated this means there isn't any)

These can be said in a monotone 'oh I am so bored tone' or a cheerful happy 'I love my job' voice or 'I REALLY want to be at home' voice

To announcements that are less frequent, such as:-

'Good morning Ladies and Gentlemen'

'Have a good day'

'I am so sorry we are held at a signal' - followed by a good description of why

On occasions we get:-

'I am sorry Ladies and Gentleman we are going to get held up through the stations' and this has then been followed by other similar announcements including 'I am really sorry about this and trust me I am just as frustrated as you because this is my last shift and I want to get home as much as you do', followed by a big sigh.

'Will you move those body parts and bags from the doors WE CAN NOT MOVE until you do'.

'I know it is very busy Ladies and Gentlemen, but you need to move away from the doors'.

'We have a teddy bear at the station, called "George" who was left home alone on the train'.

It would be handy if whoever is leaning on the doors would not' followed by 'that's better' as the trains lurches forward.

A cheerful 'hello Ladies and Gentlemen, good to have you on board and I wish you all a great day'. (Rare, VERY rare but it has happened!)

'Please remember to take all your belongings with you; your bags, coats children and pets, when you leave the train'.

And we can even get a little light entertainment on the weather:-

I do wonder whether the train drivers realise that they have the same size audience every day as a full football stadium! And they will get to speak to more people in a year than most well-known pop stars that pull in big audiences at concerts. Most people in a lifetime would not get to hold such a large audience.

You train drivers can drone on and make us all feel dead miserable or you can stay dead quiet apart from the standard announcements (or you can even avoid these).

You can cheerfully make an entire train load of dead miserable, self-absorbed commuters, smile and even laugh out loud, if you feel inclined too.

You can change someone's attitude just by saying 'rise and shine' 'good morning' to everyone 'have a great day/good evening'.

You could even sing to us if you so wished.

A big thank you to the train driver on the early morning commute who kindly told everyone 'if you are not in a hurry and you are standing, the train on the platform across from us is due to depart a couple of minutes after us if you want a seat' (the train opposite was empty). Even the commuters in the carriage were shocked into talking (commuters don't talk, Period) One saying, 'wow that was nice of the driver to tell us that'. It's happened once in the 5 years that I have travelled on this line.

Thank you to the platform staff; all those miserable commuters you get to see and talk to each and every day. You have the power to make us all even more miserable or make each and every one of us smiles through the power of talk. You have the audience the size of a small rock concert on a daily basis. You can sing your 'mind the closing doors', 'use all the available space', 'keep behind the yellow line', in whatever style you feel like, from opera to rap, or you can just make a dreary day worse.

The Hair

Oh my god the hair thing; I really would like to thank all the ladies who like to continually stroke their gorgeous long hair whether with a brush or their fingers. I love the way they can flick and faff that hair across the carriage because they believe everyone wants a piece of it like its gold dust (and we all know it may actually have been someone else's until they sold it so you can then have your fabulous mane of hair). Worse still they peel if off their hands and chuck it at whomever or whatever is nearest. I just love the way all of that hair alights its owner to join someone else as if, its running for freedom or it decides to take a look at someone else's life so it sticks itself like super glue to another's clothing. The person it then joins spends the next week extracting the ownerless hair (which is generally a completely different colour to their own and how come it is always extra-long and thick?). You will find it attached to your clothing, your bag, inside your bag or strangely it may even appear in your sandwich at lunch time or your evening dinner. Yes, it will be draped across your steak like some seductive siren waiting to be noticed, which if you are lucky you do before it ends up in your mouth and you are left extracting a never ending piece of hair from your mouth.

And let's not even think about the consequences of these ladies undertaking their grooming ritual in front of the end of carriage doors when the window is open!! That's a time to keep your MOUTH SHUT!

We really would prefer you to all undertake your personal grooming rituals in the privacy of your own home or workplace please.

How us humans love routine

We all seem to crave routine and never more so than on the underground. You know the one where you walk the same path and direction every day or where you like to stand at a certain point on the platform to board the same carriage and get the same seat (this is more for those of us who have the luxury of getting on at the end of an underground line when there are seats!). We like to go through the same exit point even though it's full of the same commuters following their own daily regular routine because it does not require any extra brain power. To change tactic and try a different route each day would mean thinking. You will see the odd break out from the herd, that one person who breaks free from the regular routine and decides to go it alone by sneaking through another route across the other platform. They are happy to make that extra effort to get to the same exit as the rest of us but quicker. What it really boils down to is conserving energy, effort, and thought. Making that break away from the herd will so upset the status quo so don't do it, just continue following the herd.

This is similar to the person who gets in the same carriage because they can (not because it's the shortest route to their exit) and they sit in the same seat. You know the ones that are nearest the door because these are easier to alight from, as they have a hand rail running horizontal to your body and can be grabbed to heave yourself up from your seat without much effort and you are out of the door before the herd has had chance to compute that they have stopped at a station. There is also the person, who at all costs will avoid sitting on any of the priority seats because they do not want to have to give up their seat when a priority seat person enters the carriage and glares down at you.

Those things on Wheels

Then you get those blasted things on wheels being pulled along by some cretin who simply does not care that they are leaving a trail of destruction in their wake as they drag that wheelie object blindly behind them. They spare no thought to anyone who has to jump like a racehorse scaling Becher's Brook at the Grand National otherwise they risk the removal of a leg has it smacks into them.

You may be the best runner within the myriad of platforms and corridors. You will move swiftly and stealthy aside to avoid the crowds surging towards you and then you realise the wheelie thing hurtling towards your legs! You do not see it because the cretin pulling the trolley has forgotten that it's behind them, as it rips into your legs catching your tights (ladies do not, I say again, do not, wear expensive hosiery on the underground because it will only last the day if you are very lucky. Make sure you have a spare pair or nicely tanned legs or stick to trousers, it's cheaper). The cretin pulling the trolley is completely unaware they are being followed by the person now attached (trapped!) to their thing on wheels, so continues on their way. You then have a choice, either stand your ground and completely lose your entire hosiery and then pretend it didn't happen and walk off, or you can run after said idiot hoping they will stop so you can extract yourself cleanly with a rather large hole or two in your hosiery (which you can then pretend are part of the design).

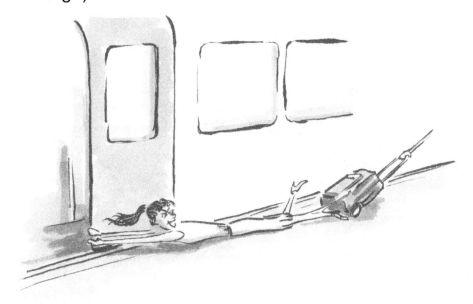

G

entleman (thankfully there are some not too scared to be one)

On the odd occasion you do have the pleasure of meeting an absolutely die hard gentleman; for example, the one who, within the crowd waiting for the underground carriage door to open, swept his arms wide parted the crowd and uttered those immortal words 'STOP we are not all in such a rush to get on this carriage that we cannot stand aside and let this elderly lady alight before us'. Strangely enough everyone stood stock still in shock that he dare utter such words and in doing so he removed everyone's auto pilot. Well, it was either that or maybe it was because he was rather a large man that they would prefer not to upset!

Thank you also to the man who knocked my shoe off; he said 'sorry' and then held the throng back from exiting the carriage and mowing me down in the process, whilst I managed to get the shoe back on. Luck was with me that day and the shoe did not fall through the crevice between the carriage and the platform, some of which require a pole-vault to get across, and would have rendered me embarrassingly shoeless for the rest of the day.

Eye lash curlers? Are you insane?

Oh my god, eye lash curlers on the move. Are you mad? Do they not know these things are dangerous and should have a health warning on them, 'DO NOT USE ON THE UNDERGROUND!' Can you imagine them getting stuck just as the person next to you slings their bag over their shoulder (you know, one of those massive great back packs that probably contain just a packed lunch and a drink, because surely most people now have small mobile devices, and not those laptops which weigh the same as small elephant from a bygone age?). It knocks the arm that is busy holding the contraption which apparently curls your lashes and makes them look longer (not sure how because they just cause a kink to appear in your lashes so they look like they have been folded over) and suddenly the curler is still in your hand, still with lashes enclosed however they are no longer attached to your eye. You now have a bald eye which you then try to style out pretending it was all intentional. You will now have to stop off to get some super glue or wait to see if they will grow back! Or maybe your hand became disengaged from the curling contraption (difficult because you generally have your thumb and finger stuck in the scissor handles) and the curling machine is now stuck to your eye lashes which are thankfully still attached in their rightful place however you now look like a complete halfwit with this contraption swinging from your lashes whilst you chase it around your face without drawing too much attention to yourself, (either that or you pretend you meant to leave the curlers swinging from your lashes whilst you dive into that huge makeup bag for another torturous contraption in the aid of beauty). Little wonder those handbags are so huge ladies! You then manage to disengage said curlers but in doing so realise your stop went passed about ten minutes ago!

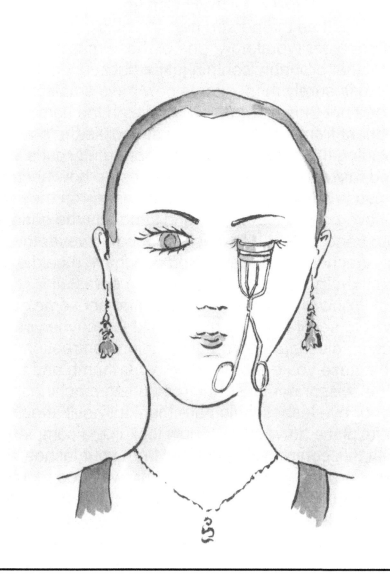

The husband and wife routine

The husband and wife team; you know, the kind who get on the same carriage and sit in the same seats together, the wife then provides the husband with a newspaper first and foremost and then produces one for herself. They do not say a word whilst reading those papers; they do not comment about what is in the papers, no small chat, not a glance or a small touch of the hand. You then of course start to imagine their life and you always come up with some boring, even tempered, non-exciting life of making the tea day in day out, (chips and egg Monday, lasagne Tuesday, salad Wednesday, steak Thursday down the pub after work on Friday!), mowing the lawn and washing the car on Saturday morning, golf in the afternoon for the husband and shopping for the wife and maybe they still have grown up children at home (on the average assumption of 2 children and a dog). By now you are yawning and have got bored with the life of Mr and Mrs Average who each day travel to the station together (never late) getting the same underground train, standing in the same area of the platform, to get in the same underground carriage, to get the same seats, the wife produces a newspaper for the husband first from her bag and then one for herself. I get to see them doing this each day I travel in the same carriage and sit in the same seat until I get bored with that and decide to see who is in the next carriage doing the same thing each and every day.

The Leg Crosser

How about people who cross their legs swinging those legs across the gap between the seats and then expect no one to move and fill up all that space?; someone then shouts 'move up and use all available space' and everyone moves up in between the seating but what do you do with the leg and foot that is in the way because the leg crosser thinks they are in a cosy sofa arrangement like their front room? Do you soldier through ignoring their leg and foot that makes no effort to move? It then continues to swing and jog with the movement of the underground carriage smacking you in some part of your body (this is dependent on how tall you are). So then you gently remind them by a small movement or body twist then it turns into a war of wits because they just move a little to the side (hopefully you are not stride that foot and leg and end up riding it like a rocking horse!).

If you are a stride it you could do the leg crosser manoeuvre and grip that dammed leg and foot so hard and make for the exit door pretending not to notice that the leg crosser has been dragged from their seat, hit the carriage floor, banged their head, crashed through the door onto the platform where you release them and turn around offering perfuse apologies and kindly help them off the floor.

The other option is to fall backwards, crush the foot that is on the floor with your full body weight, which immediately releases the crossed leg whilst you smile sweetly and say 'oh I am so sorry I do apologise'.

Claiming that seat

We seasoned commuters know where to position ourselves on the underground carriage and have the knowledge of which station is going to deposit most of the people who are all sat directly behind and in front of you, whilst you straddle that area between the seats. You then expand yourself width ways to make yourself look a lot bigger than you are so that you have the option to take either the two seats behind you or the two in front if any of these are vacated at the any of the stations coming next. You are like a hunter watching every single movement from those four people (note if they are sleeping they are not going to move until the end of the line and you do not want to be sat next to a sleeper unless you like them head butting your shoulder or just falling into your lap. Strangely they never EVER fall forward into their own laps or head butt the floor or the crotch that is stood directly in front of them). The seasoned commuter has the hunter instinct watching all movements from the four sitters, the slight movement of the hand, the glance at the tube map, the shift of position, the closing of the book, the decisive collecting of the bag, (or whatever paraphernalia they have about them). The hunter then starts to prepare themselves for the best way to seize that seat before anyone else has even noticed its occupant has vacated. They either, quietly manoeuvre themselves into position without attracting the attention of the opposition, or just stand directly in front of the soon to be vacated seat blocking all entrances from the front left and right sides. You do this whilst always looking fairly relaxed as not to draw attention to your actions (this is to be avoided at all costs whilst travelling on the underground). It is all going to plan until just before the station the person you have been stalking stands up directly in front of you. They head butt you in the process because just for that second you are distracted by their sudden movement, forgetting momentarily that a swift movement to the left (or right dependent on the sitters exit strategy) was required to enable the sitter to squeeze passed you whilst you took procession of the vacant seat. The head butt is a stinging blow that takes a second or two to recover from but once you've recovered you present smiles all round as you don't want to bring attention to the fact that you feel like you have just had your opponent, the sitter, nearly knock you out cold in your quest to take procession of the vacant seat. Unfortunately, during your recovery seconds, the person to your left seizes the opportunity and stealthy sits down whilst you are left counting the stars.

The hunter starts the process again whilst trying to cover the large bump that has now started to appear on their forehead. The next time they are able to hang on to the top handrail whilst swinging to the left to the let the sitter exit their seat. This enables the hunter to swing round, let go of the handrail and fall into the vacant seat without falling into the person on either side. By the time the hunter finally gets a seat the bump is clearly visible for all to see.

The Sauna

It was a stifling humid day during a British summer time though the sky was grey, and it was raining.

This combination is all well and good up top but not in the depths of the underground where the atmosphere is more a kin to a sauna. There are certainly a few trains which pretend to have air-conditioning and a few which actually do. I normally end up on the ones that are like large metal cooking pots (think of a tin can, in boiling water, with you in it!). So throughout the summer it is such a joy because you never ever need to pay to visit any type of sauna to sweat out all those toxins. You can just use your everyday commute on the underground to emulate a sauna. One time I readily stepped on to the underground carriage, one of those hot tin cans and felt a cool back draft of air conditioning. I stopped slightly dazed because it was actually cool on this carriage. I was confused; I thought that I must be on the wrong train, so promptly got off to check I was on the right platform!

The Baby Badge

Once in an utter state of startled shock (or that's what I am blaming my mistake on), because I actually got a seat on a packed underground carriage, I was busy reading and suddenly noted this small protruding stomach directly in front of my face so I immediately offered my seat up but the lady owner of said protruding stomach declined and I realised this protruding stomach was not a pregnant protruding stomach! Oh dear! I hung my head in shame and carried on reading whilst the lady in question wrapped her coat around her protruding stomach. I then stupidly make some effort to rectify my mistake by saying 'sorry I thought I saw a baby badge' (she clearly was not wearing one). At this point I realise there was a language barrier and did the daft thing of repeating myself, to which her friend then cottoned on to what I was saying and started laughing. Her friend then, I am assuming, proceeded to tell her friend. At this point I gave up although was tempted to follow it with a 'wow you must of eaten a lot of bread today' and went back to my reading. Embarrassed in my mistake I promised myself in future to look for a baby badge first and foremost no matter how big the stomach!

The overriding rule is that you need to be careful here otherwise you may end up giving up that precious seat to someone who has wind! Look for the badge at all times to avoid the embarrassment (generally yours)

The man in the eye mask

Why would you want to completely block out all your senses, so you do not get the delight of seeing, hearing and smelling the underground carriages? I mean surely you want to listen to all of the conversations the other commuters have (rarely do seasoned commuters have any conversations unless they know you will not have a clue what they are saying and then do this at the highest decibels possible or they want to show off and talk jargon thinking they sound so intelligent (they don't) or they want you to hear their grand holiday/travel plans, or if you are lucky you will get to hear all the music that is being played into someone's ears because they are so obviously deaf - why else would you play it that loud?

And then we have the smells; at the start of the day there is highly scented perfumed and aftershave and then towards the end of the day there are the less favourable smells, which you tend to avoid at all costs but this isn't always, especially when you have the pleasure of a stranger's armpit or other body part directly under your nose. I am not sure which is worse, an arm pit in your face, someone's crutch or a derriere!! God knows what it is like when you are less than five-foot-tall because you will constantly have one or all of these in your face.

Then there are all the wonderful sights you would miss; the miserable commuters all dressed in black with the odd splash of black!

However, the person who decided to do his home commute with his ears plugged up to a mega ear music set and eye mask obviously had decided enough was enough. The only thing that was missing was a nose peg!

Commuter Face

There are times when the facade of the seasoned commuters face can cause offence or embarrassment and should not be used in all instances because - a small smile works wonders along with good manners and brings out the best in people. If you do crack your poker face facade to another seasoned commuter that in turn cracks their facade because they think 'oh my god there is another human on this carriage' and they will mirror back the smile (short, sharp and quick, so has not to be seen by another!)

My seasoned commuter face caused a young man, who was sat opposite and had been watching me with intent, some embarrassment. When I looked up and gave him my best seasoned commuter face. Well I was then mortified for the rest of my journey because that young man was so filled with embarrassment that I had caught him watching me and he looked like he wanted a big hole to open and swallow him up! So, lesson learnt, smile because we are all interested in others and people watching, I believe, is one of the most prized pastimes (it's also free!). Also, the London Underground is one of the best places to do it. Of course, if we want to be miserable blighters then the London Underground is also the best place to do it too!

Grooming Rituals

I am still waiting to see that one person (because we know it's coming after all people use the underground carriage to undertake nearly all their own personal grooming rituals),to travel in their bedroom attire bringing along their arm pit sprays, hair grooming kits, make up bags, tooth brushes and their business attire. They can then set up their own bathroom suite (on the seat next to them on the underground carriage) and proceed to show the rest of the underground carriage their morning rituals (no toilet opportunities here), all because they were to dammed lazy to get out of their bed early and do their bum scratching, nose picking, bodily functions, grooming, shower and dressing, in their own bathroom!

Putting arm pit protection (deodorant) on in front of everyone, the shame! I mean, did this woman get up that late that she rushed out only stopping to pick up a can of deodorant instead of having a shower? By spraying her pits in public, she proceeded to show everyone she had forgotten to wash? Did she not realise the underground carriage was actually full of people and it really seriously was not her own bathroom? Or did she think all commuters were so dazed that no one would even notice? Well I did!

Part of a Group Hug

Some commuters can be extremely friendly and will involve you in their conversations, even though you are a complete stranger. They will engage you in conversations that are completely random however please note this engagement stops as soon as they and their colleagues or friends exit the carriage, so be aware you will not always get the entire conversation unless you follow them (creepy). You must also be aware it does not require you to utter one word to either party who are engaged in the conversation - I love the fact you can be stood directly in the middle of two people (who you do not know), whilst an entire conversation is taking place and you just have to listen.

I was party to a conversation just because I was stood between two commuters and whilst I was swinging around the hand rail they merrily included me in their conversation about their next holiday destination (Maldives) and how great their previous holiday had been (Dubai). I have been included in a conversation between two commuters who were discussing the best place to buy a house, where and how to get the best mortgage, how much their current properties were worth and whether they should keep or sell and move on. I have heard girls talking about their successful or unsuccessful weekend/party night out, how much they had drunk, whether they had 'copped' off with some minger and then the complete opposite but same conversation between two men (all very entertaining). I have been party to conversations between two young ladies and learned of their debt mountain and who were the best money loan sharks to hook up with. I stand there nodding and looking captivated just so I feel part of their conversation because I am sandwiched between them with nowhere to go. Of course most of the time we all stay dead

145

quiet looking utterly miserable or pretend to be engaged in other things such as reading the paper, our phones, listening to music, putting underarm deodorant on, picking our nose, or sharing makeup and ones hair with everyone within 5 feet.

The Seat Giver

It is always interesting when you are in a packed to the rafters carriage where you are squashed up close to bodies you would rather not be and a gentleman in the priority seat on the carriage offers you their seat but because you know in the next couple of stops the train is going to empty fairly rapidly you politely offer your thanks and decline. Then you glance around and see others who he could have offered his seat to and then you think, ummmm why me? Oh my god did he think I was pregnant? I knew I shouldn't have had that rather large lunch earlier as you look down stealthily (so no one notices) to check out the stomach which I have already start to draw in. How embarrassing! Then after talking myself into the fact that my stomach looks nice and flat, so it wasn't that, I then begin to wonder, did he think I had passed the age of sixty-five? Nope, I checked for grey hairs this morning and I know I had a tough day at work but last time I looked I certainly had not gained twenty years (or maybe I think I look young and everyone else sees me differently!?). So, after a process of elimination I come to the conclusion this nice young gentleman had offered his seat just out of plain old fashioned, wonderful common politeness and what a marvellous person he was for doing just that!

To all the men that are gracious enough to give your seat up for a lady I say, 'thank you'. Trust me when you do this, no matter how old or young you are, how you are dressed, what work you do, or why you are even on the carriage, for me it will be seen has extremely gracious and kind so I will always offer you a big smile and a very kind thank you because for me it is so dammed polite. And please, if I refuse to take your kind offer you do not need to apologise and say, 'I did not mean to offend you'.

I have had long conversations with an entire rail engineering team who were visiting and working from the north because one insisted, I take his seat. (Apologies to anyone travelling on this carriage because we were talking!)

Giving your seat to a woman with a very young child? How young? A baby? A toddler? or a teenager?

What about a child who looks about ten years old, someone who is more capable of standing than you are? So, what do you do if the mother asks you to give up your seat for said child? Do you ignore her feigning sudden deafness or lack of English? Do you begrudgingly give up your seat crying and screaming as you cling on to it slowly relinquishing it to said child, or do you say 'are you kidding me? Seriously? I have advancing years my body has had thirty years of abuse I am treble the age of your child and that child has less weight to carry', then return to your reading!

Those winter coats

It is strange how the commuter species has great difficulty shedding its winter coats; it can be blue sky, sunshine and mid-summer and yet in the depths of the underground you will see many of the fully suited and booted resiliently holding on to their winter layers. That overcoat that needs to go to the cleaners which has been your staple wear throughout the winter months that believe me is not required in July. Ladies you can also ditch the thick black tights you'll just have to shave a little more often. Please fill the underground with summer colours and men in their summer gear, t-shirt and shorts (ok maybe not the shorts) you don't need to hold on to that dull thick winter coat release it and give it to the dry cleaners go on you can do it!

The gum chewer

Is it just me or is there something incredibly unattractive to be sat in a packed carriage of dreary commuter's chewing gum with their mouths wide open and smacking those lips together? This can be either sexes and is just as unattractive in both, or maybe I just don't understand that they like to share their entire gum chewing experience with the rest of us by keeping their mouth open whilst chucking the piece of white stuff around and around. You follow it round memorised, like watching a washing machine, trying to guess what that thing is going around and around. Then because you are getting such a clear tunnel vision straight into that black hole you realise it is a piece of chewed up gum (we are on the underground carriage here so you have no option but to get up close and personal to that very open mouth in fact the way these open mouth chewers operate generally ensures everyone gets a clear view of that opened mouth and anything in it. I suppose it does entertain the rest of us less uncouth dreary lot and we get to watch how unattractive all that scenery is in there, so we make sure we keep our mouths very shut. I mean if there were flies down in the underground (strangely there isn't and yet flies appear everywhere else, maybe they have more sense than to travel via the underground or they know something we don't!) then you would get to spend time watching how many flies end up in those open mouths and how they would get stuck in the gum!!

Coughing Should be Banned

Oh my god what a racket just listen to that coughing; she is going to infect everyone with a mortal disease. You can see everyone looking worried (for their own health not the person who is coughing their guts up) You can see them going through a list of all the fatal diseases that involve a heavy cough as they move further away (which isn't far because they are rammed up against everyone else who are now googling coughing diseases). Someone kindly offers the perpetrator a sweet which they readily take, the coughing stops, and everyone breathes a sigh of relief and the carriage goes back to normal.

The Long Brolly Brigade

The brolly attack! you have to be aware of the long brolly brigade on the underground. You know the ones that carry those long fixed full sized brollies that are dangerous even when above ground (great in the rain and a gale force wind, which you don't get in the underground – ok so maybe the occasional gust when you descend the escalators or stairs and then you lose that lovely loose flowing skirt because it ends up round your ears). Now those brollies can end up wrapped around the owner's legs because they have no idea how to carry them along with all the other paraphernalia they carry around. If you stand anywhere within three foot of these things with an owner that doesn't have a clue you will end up poked and prodded, so have your guard up. These will come at you like a sharp right hook and take your eye out so you will need to undertake the deep dive bend backwards duck defence like your life depends on it. You may look like you are in a Kung Fu movie, but it beats getting poked by those blasted brollies.

If you are sat and someone is trying to contain one of those brollies when everyone sprints towards the empty seat on your right, you will need to block it with your bag otherwise it's going to end up in your rib cage or up your nose! Do NOT EVER walk directly behind someone with one of these brollies because trust me the owner will shove it under their arm pit and your eye will be speared on the end of it. Whilst on an escalator give the brolly at least ten steps of space because when it gets you it will be like a domino reaction and a pile of commuters will end up detangling themselves from the mess at the bottom.

The water bottle

So, after travelling throughout a number of summer months without a bright spark idea let me tell you about the best ever ninety pence I spent EVER!

All seasoned commuters know the worse train/tube lines to travel on in the summer, so I really have no need to enlighten you, on how it is possible to lose 10lb by just stepping inside one of these metal tins. You will have sweated out all those toxins from the last ten years in a matter of minutes. We know when the temperature outside has reached 30 degrees the underground will be 100 degrees and the underground carriages will be 1000 degrees. The bodies which you will invariably be squashed up against will be wet, sticky and hot but at least you will 'pop out' easily when your exit appears. Now we also know that trying to fan yourself with any magazine or newspaper (that is thrown at you before you descend into the depths of the underground) is a waste of time because you are just moving that 1000 degree air around a little. So before you descend, arm yourself with a bottle of water you have just purchased above ground from the back of the fridge (make an extra effort and get the bottle from the very back of the fridge otherwise you may find within ten minutes its boiling). DO NOT DRINK IT, but as soon as you get into the metal cooking pot place that oh so cold water bottle against your neck, face, forehead and you will think that you are in heaven. Oh the joy, the coolness close your eyes and just feel that cold amazing immediate body temperature drop - a joy and an instant sweat deterrent. There is only one downside (apart from spending the 90 pence and having to divert your journey planner slightly) everyone in that metal cooking pot will be staring at you wishing they had that same bright idea whilst you continue to look perfectly cool.

The Urinal

I am certain urinals are generally white, roundish and stuck to a wall within a toilet? So I was at a loss when I stepped onto the empty underground carriage at the end of the line, first thing in the morning, to see a man stood up in the same stance has a man having a pee. I thought 'no there is no urinal in this carriage so I must be mistaken' so I sat down some distance from the man in question and proceeded to read the Metro. Then it hit me, the strong and very unpleasant smell of a VERY unclean public toilet, so I looked across at said man who was sitting down at this time and again thought 'NO surely not?, He surely had undertaken his bathroom ritual before leaving his house? Maybe a dog had cocked its leg before I got on the carriage?' So I carried on reading the paper trying not to breath too much, and you know us commuters, we don't want to have to move from our usual position of same carriage, same seat, do we? So, I steadfastly remained in MY seat, stopped breathing and then I looked down and saw this yellow water running towards my feet like a tidal wave. 'OH MY GOD HE PEED IN THIS CARRIAGE'! I shot out of my seat like it had set my bottom on fire and out of the door, nearly knocking the station attendant over whilst I shouted 'you will need a peg for your nose, a mop and bucket because that man does not know the different between a underground carriage and a urinal'!

The end

EPILOGUE

Lastly I would like to offer my VERY sincere thanks to all the underground train drivers who get us to and from work each and every day; To the station staff who put up with us miserable commuters and yet always remain polite; To the cleaners who pick up after us lazy miserable lot and the entire network of workers who keep this massive behemoth moving and get all those commuters every single day spilling out of this dark mass of labyrinth of underground tunnels to the light above

Thank you to all of the travelling public who use this behemoth to circumnavigate London without whom I would not have had the opportunity to write this book.

To all of you who brave the underground without the same mobility has some of us I absolutely SALUTE you because the commuter brigade will unintentionally try and plough through you come what may so let me apologise on their behalf!

*

Printed in Great Britain
by Amazon